Melanie Shudofsky

THE ART OF BEING

THE ART OF BEING
Awakening to your Inner Guide

Copyright © 2019 by Melanie Shudofsky

The illustrations included in this book are from the author. Information about the location and date of the photo taken can be read on the last pages of this book.

First Edition

For information about special discounts available for bulk purchases, sales promotions, fund-raising and educational needs, contact the author Melanie Shudofsky through the website: **www.melanieshudofsky.com.**

All Rights Reserved

No portion of this book may be produced in any form or transmitted in any form by any means –electronic, mechanical, photocopy, recording, or otherwise –without permission from the publisher, except as permitted by U.S. copyright law. For permission requests, contact the publisher through: **www.melanieshudofsky.com.**

ISBN: 978-1-7333112-1-2

THE ART OF BEING

Awakening to your Inner Guide

Melanie Shudofsky

Who am I in this very moment?

Do I see that which is my true Self?

1.

The sudden change takes place right in that moment when one thinks it cannot go any further.

One expects the cool breeze, but it is the lazy heat which calms it down. The fullness which at first seems to dominate slowly appears to be a companion. A stop line seems at first definite and limiting, but it actually provides the chance to see more. That which one thinks is possible to define changes at the first word into something fluid.

There is always that change; unexpected, undefinable, a companion which helps one to see more.

2.

Listen and it will tell.

If one does not listen, it will show.

If the eyes are blurred, it will make you feel.

Senses absorbed, it will shut everything down.

To move on or to stand still.

3.

What is it that drives us?

What makes us live the life like we do?

4.

Every encounter is taken along, stays, gets a place. No matter how short the encounter. No matter how fleeting. Added. The more intimate the deeper it settles. A small plant sometimes travels along for the duration of a lifetime.

An expression, a touch, a gesture, a word – spoken, written, thought of.

5.

There is nothing we can actually hold onto. Like embracing a cloud: it becomes a part of you but at the same time it is not tangible. It has a certain influence but at the same time it is not easily described. Try to hold onto it and it will let go. Like the air bubbles on the water surface: a part of yourself you find in the reflection, but touch it and it will dissolve.

Many words spoken can have the same effect as wanting to embrace the clouds or touching the air bubbles on the water surface.

Behold without will or reason and the beauty remains. The answers given.

6.

One thought can be as strong as the physical world itself.

7.

A traveler.

Always on the move.

In different ways and in different forms.

Moving within the perception of someone else.

On our way on our two feet which take us further.

On our way by being quiet and turning inwards.

On our way by observing the world around us and to see the changes moving before our eyes.

A traveler.

The world within and without.

8.

Still water. The reflection no longer clear. Wind moves it not. The sun hardens the surface. Slowly evaporating. A last small puddle. Sand covers the remains. Until the breaking of clouds by a thunder and lightning struck sky.

9.

The experience determines the direction.

10.

Only the steps in front of her exist. Breathing in the same rhythm. There is no down below and to quit is no option. Step by step in the same rhythm. To be able to continue. To move forward. Pure mountain air inhaling with every breath.

11.

How the new enriches. Even though it is not always easy. Like a storm with heavy rains and pulling wind, lightning and thunder. It would seem best to stay inside. Wait a moment. Be patient. Slowly the thunder resolves, more and more towards the distance. Between the palm trees it seems as if it is still raining. Drops slide off the leaves. The soil takes it in eagerly. Everything seems even more green.

Take it in and take it along. Observe and listen. Let it be and continue. Do with it what you can. How the new enriches.

Watch it come and let it go. In movement although sitting. It settles slowly although one is only watching. The water flows undisturbed, finds its way. There are no obstacles, only a flowing through the path of least resistance.

How the new enriches.

12.

Sometimes three steps back are needed to enable a leap forward.

13.

Nothingness. Gravel plains and sand dunes as far as the eye can see and beyond. Little trees stand like a rock against the dry elements.

Nothingness. Everything is in movement. Loud whistling of the wind. It takes it along and shapes the desert. It does not have a goal, it only knows the direction.

Everything is in movement. There is no beginning. There is no ending. One moment leads to the next. One takes it along and the other changes it.

A black crow flies high above a sand tornado. The bright sun reflects on its wings. One moment later it disappears into the nothingness. Humans and nature each reflect time in their own way. Humans want to pin up, plan, assure. Put a drawing pin into the moment and hang it on the wall. Assured. The passing of time in nature reflected in the changing of the landscape. What has been, has passed.

The following of the wind. Everything is in movement.

Nothingness. There is so much to see.

14.

Follow the subtle.

See where it originates.

Sense where it stops.

Adapt accordingly.

15.

Just try.

16.

How spontaneous encounters with strangers while being surrounded by the wonders of nature can bring us in awe. And with the ease of a breath of wind they can bring us back to the Source within.

How experiences on the Way can make our Being grow and deepen and at the same time these experiences provide replenishment.

How being on the Way resolves the questions and bring forward clarity, answers and confirmations. A reflection in the eyes of someone else, in the flowing of the water, in the stranger who gives without expecting something in return, in a condor flying high above during climbing.

The unchangeable Being above the coming and going.

17.

A corn poppy flower alongside the with traffic jam filled road. Slowly forming clouds of thunder change the sky into grey. Standing still on the tar. The road which takes one further. A stork with her nest on an electricity pylon.

Shaping time in a conscious manner; staying aware of the Way which fits one best. It is a continuous forming of ideas, images and quiet awareness which can make the feeling arise that it fits. What is needed to continue growing; that one can experience all that is possible.

A place is left behind for moving towards the next goal, for the next steps.

Everyone is on the road in their own way. A hiking trail through the mountains, ideas and wishes for the future, the emptiness of a moment, the exit to another city, a hawk hovering above the traffic jam filled road.

18.

A memory which was linked to a different context. Brought forward into a new decor. The newness of the moment intertwines. Like the morning mist through the forest. The rising sun slowly makes it disappear.

Remain observant with clear eyes. Embracing the new and let the old be.

19.

Even slowing down means movement.

20.

Many layers. Everywhere. Always. It does not matter where one is.

Take a boat and sail with that what your eyes can see. Change course according to the current. Small adjustments. Small movements.

When the water approaches then dive in or take a step back.

Like a painting the sky changes. Little by little a brush stroke is added.

Subtle change in every layer.

21.

Caught up in a life situation, one still has the ability to make changes, no matter how small. Therefore it is not the ability, but the seeing, knowing and doing of what is possible.

22.

When traveling towards our true Self, mostly the roads within ourselves will provide us with answers. The people we encounter on the way are like a reflection in the mountain lake: they are not the answer themselves but can provide clarity along the journey.

23.

Those steps which are not directly explainable in words are naturally the steps which fit best with who one truly is. Try to describe it and it will lose value.

What seems contradictory on the surface but what feels like a truth in the undercurrent, that is our Inner Guide that leads us. The Inner Guide is what remains when thoughts are not dominating.

Who says that it is easy?

Continuously we are influenced by the many voices surrounding us. Telling us what would be best for us. Listen, bring it along or let it go. Inner guidance is always present, but it is up to ourselves to fine tune with it.

What seems contradictory on the surface but what feels like the truth in the undercurrent, that is the Way. Where it will take us is the great adventure of life. A continuous discovery of our boundaries and the possibilities to push these boundaries. Defy every wave, knowing to be anchored in our true Self.

24.

Sometimes only little is needed to change a lot.

25.

And that is how we keep moving. In connection with many elements.

Similarities in visions and thoughts, added with words.

Insight moves along with the flowing stream. Nourished by that which lies at the river bank. Enriched and challenged by that which blends with the water.

It is the continuous alternation of acceleration and slowing down which makes us grow.

Intensity in the movement alternated with reflection in the calmness.

And through this we remain in touch with the many elements within ourselves and without.

We keep moving.

26.

Observing the life. A bird's eye view of steps tracing back. There where it once began. The mixing of worlds which gave birth to the soul of the traveler. A comfortable alienation from the daily rhythm. Recognizing what is needed to expand.

27.

Commitment lasts as long as the elements surrounding it allow.

28.

People come and go. Receive and take and leave again. Watch and give and move away again.

It is our own Way on which we will have to focus. One can dwell on the other, help to gain insight and provide support, but it is our own Way which we have to guard. When we are moving on our true path, then we will also be able to give without expecting something in return, to support the other and do what is right for the world in which we live. Alignment with who we truly are can only bring beautiful manifestations.

29.

Change is coming. Almost tangible, like the morning mist.

Looking around it all seems the same. A soft blanket of grey surrounding the green. But somewhere within, change has begun to form. Almost tangible, like the sound of morning mist.

30.

What makes one feel a thorough enjoyment independent of anything specific?

31.

To have a goal in mind, no matter how small or big. Subsequently letting go of it so other experiences on the way can be allowed and embraced in all its forms.

One can draw fixed lines, but every event and every experience only takes shape in the moment itself. This seems rather logical, but too often one assumes to know everything beforehand; to be able to predict it all.

Leave the coloring of the lines to the moment itself.

32.

Sometimes it is better to wait for the rain to stop.

But sometimes it is even better to just dive in.

33.

The way it came it also leaves. Creeping, silently, but nevertheless noticeable. A blow here and a thug there. Slowly space expands within the Self, and between people. Space in the whole.

The empty spaces are easily filled. But it is the empty space which we need in order to see.

The way it came it also disappears. Creeping, silently, but nevertheless noticeable. As a small compensation for the resistance. As a small gift for letting go.

Step into the empty space and breath in. See what is.

Step into the fullness of the moment and breath out. See what comes and goes.

The continuous changing as the one factor connecting us all.

34.

Take a breath. Float above the substance. Let it go. See what is left.

35.

It is the Art of Being to be silently aware. To see beyond the conditioned tasks and thoughts. To listen beyond the many words which we have to process every day. If we leave those for what they are, and move our attention to the silence, then we come closer to our true Self and the purity of that what is present in our lives.

Connect with it, that silence within yourself, and every step will be taken consciously and in alignment with who you truly are, who you actually would like to be and what you wish to achieve.

With every step it will become more clear, that which you need for your next step. Keep your focus, but don't care too much about it. Like the Buddha who smiles. Disciplined but just as well moving along like the heaving waves at sea.

36.

It is everywhere, visible, tangible but it cannot be explained.

37.

Clouds are forming, sunrays pierce through. The green vivid on the mountain, as if you can breathe in every detail. Fresh air here above. The heat reflects on the ocean water there below. Realizing there are so many beautiful small things being brought forward, in between the challenges of those things which are complex.

With every step towards altitude, heaviness getting stronger in the legs, but lighter and lighter within.

38.

The world is the way it is. Until the next encounter.

39.

Accepting that the feeling will not change. It indicates she must not stay. It is the place in between two chains. A moment to set basics and prepare for what will come next.

40.

Do I see that which is?

Maybe I only see what I want to see.

41.

Slowly.

A single breath.

Taking it in.

A moment filled by emptiness itself.

42.

Not to be in a life situation only because one stopped to really see; too much swallowed up by the everyday actions.

43.

Nothing else can exist. Only the movement in the moment. The balancing of the mind. The strength of focus. A brush of wind. Tension is released. Enabling the next movement. The step taken characterized by the strength of the mind.

44.

A certain desolation and the freedom to choose for and to immerse in it.

45.

One step closer. Closer to what?

A perception of what is. Or a perception of what is not.

We decide when we arrive.

The way we see determines what we will find.

46.

Is this step necessary or just something for in between?

47.

It comes and it goes.

The warmth closes it in, the wind pushes it out.

Within the continuous unrest lies the rest, within the movement lies the calmness.

Small plants with deep roots.

To move on or to stay.

48.

A life full of possibilities; for some a fact for others just a dream.

49.

The warmth of friendship.

He waits and looks out onto the field.

Just a glimpse of what could be.

Just wait and one will see.

The life changing touch of purity.

50.

With every step many worlds come together.

51.

Slowly pushing towards a certain direction.

Events arise. Questions answered and confirmed. The Way takes its course. Is this the road to take?

One step leads to another. A gesture, a word, an image. The direction is shown.

See the Way reflected within.

52.

A recurrent rhythm. Chosen by ourselves or by the will of others. What would you choose?

53.

With every breath it resolves. That which lies down below. Lighter in her thoughts, heavier in her legs which carry her forward. There is only one Way. The beauty of nature surrounds her; it is in every detail. That which lies below she abandons, symbolized by the cover of clouds below.

54.

Living slowly in the moment itself. Living fast in the whole. The opportunity to discover and to learn.

55.

Do you see the clouds moving?

56.

That which seems empty is filled.

The still is fluid.

Sounds make silence exist.

The body heated up by the cold.

57.

Am I happy with where I am?

Is there another way?

58.

Patiently looking.

Experiencing and enduring.

Streams come together.

Form a new whole.

The mixing of worlds with new perspectives as the result.

The slow stream of that which is yet to come.

59.

The dark makes the light shine even brighter; one cannot exist without the other.

60.

Slowly but steadily she passes the others. Each of them absorbed in their own rhythm. Only the steps exist and the elements of the mountain taking hold of who we are. We are incredibly small. There is no down below. She can only move forward. The cold of the wind makes her body shiver. The moonlight guides her way.

61.

Deepening of that which is already present and discovery of that which is still unknown.

62.

Take it in. Give it space.

Breathe out. Watch it evolve.

The fullness will get lighter.

Isn't there always a relieving breath within the tension?

63.

Sometimes by traveling far one discovers where one wants to be.

64.

When one is in the everyday life and the other finds herself as a traveler in a new world, then through that they will connect. Both open up their worlds for one another and for a moment they share the journey. The rest dissolves. For the one, her world feels like something far away, abstract but inseparable from who she is. Abstract because only a few facets are brought forward. As if one shows an adapted version of a table of contents depending on the reference of the other. And that makes traveling as the sowing together of two different worlds. The tangible blends with thoughts, images and ideas. And at the same time something new arises. Something, a world which only exists between the one and the other. The traveler and the local. Not long after, it dissolves into something new. The encounter as something small added to the world of the one and the world of the other.

65.

How come we communicate the way we do?

66.

Restlessness in the stillness.

Quietness in the movement.

Nothing much seems to happen.

But the whole earth is moving.

67.

Giving in.

Take a step back.

68.

The heat of the tropic sun. Big leafed trees provide the shade.

Another world intertwines. Images of the cold and vastness.

Feeling the soaring heat. Seeing the other world.

69.

Many steps in a life. Every step like a bridge between that which has been and that which is yet to come.

70.

Time seems to stand still while the everyday life is moving on. Increased awareness regarding several elements, the rest follows its own way.

It lies within our own hands. A decision here is a consequence there.

Sometimes just waiting patiently with increased awareness is the way to see the direction.

71.

Much goes lost in communication alone.

72.

She is here but the Energy has already moved on. In preparation for what is next. She is still here but in alignment with both worlds; woven into each other.

73.

A continuous coming and going.

74.

Ripples on the water. With every turn a different view. Modern navigation. The cool air welcomes us. A blanket of clouds slides across the hills. The evening light colours soft pink until darkness has fallen. The familiarity of being together but in new surroundings. The feeling of being home away from home. Slowly the water surface settles. The view more clear. The Way is shown by itself.

Photograph Details

Page 6: Bolivia, Rurrenabaque, Alto Beni; 2012

Page 9: Namibia, Namib Desert; 2015

Page 12: Switzerland, Lenk, Leiterli; 2017

Page 15: India, Rajasthan; 2014

Page 16: Indonesia, Sumatra, Kalianda; 2018

Page 19: Malaysia, Borneo, Mount Kinabalu NP; 2019

Page 22: Oman, Wahiba Sands; 2010

Page 25: Indonesia, Sumatra, Rajabasa; 2019

Page 26: Chile, El Cajón del Maipo; 2018

Page 29: Namibia, Mariental; 2015

Page 30: Indonesia, Java, Borobudur; 2018

Page 34: Switzerland, Lobhörner; 2016

Page 36: Switzerland, Lenk, Flueseeli; 2016

Page 39: Switzerland, Lenk, Rezligletscher; 2016

Page 41: Switzerland, Sanetschsee; 2017

Page 42: Switzerland, Col du Pillon; 2017

Page 45: Bolivia, Titicaca; 2012

Page 46: Switzerland, Simmental; 2017

Page 50: Chile, Aguas del Ramon; 2018

Page 54: Switzerland, Miroir d'Argentine, Route 'Remix'; 2017

Page 57: Oman, Ash Shuwaymiyyah, Wadi; 2017

Page 61: Chile, Termas del Flaco; 2018

Page 62: Malaysia, Sabah, Tunku Abdul Rahman Park; 2019

Page 65: Switzerland, Solalex, Miroir d'Argentine; 2017

Page 66: Switzerland, Zweisimmen, Sparemoos; 2017

Page 69: Malaysia, Borneo, Mount Kinabalu; 2019

Page 70: Switzerland, Leukerbad, Daubenhorn; 2018

Page 73: Switzerland, Grindelwald, Eiger,
  Route Mittellegi Ridge; 2016

Page 74: Namibia, Namib-Naukluft NP; 2015

Page 79: Chile, Cajón del Maipo; 2018

Page 83: Switzerland, Zweisimmen; 2018

Page 85: Malaysia, Sabah, Mount Kinabalu, Via Ferrata Lowe's Circuit

Page 86: Switzerland, Wallis, Zinalrothorn, Route Rothorn

Page 91: Namibia, Keetmanshoop, Giant's Playground; 2015

Page 92: Switzerland, Saanenland, Arnensee; 2017

Page 97: Switzerland, Berner Oberland, Mönch,
  Route Northeast Face; 2016

Page 98: Switzerland, Zweisimmen, Seebergsee; 2017

Page 101: Iran, Howraman Valley; 2018

Page 104: Indonesia, Flores, Padar Island; 2019

Page 107: Switzerland, Zweisimmen; 2017

Page 110: Switzerland, Zweisimmen; 2018

Page 113: Switzerland, Jaunpass; 2017

Page 114: Switzerland, Gorge de Jorge; 2017

Page 117: Switzerland, Lenk, Rezligletscher; 2016

Page 119: Indonesia, Sumatra, Kalianda; 2019

www.ingramcontent.com/pod-product-compliance
Lightning Source LLC
Chambersburg PA
CBHW041219070526
44584CB00001B/9